The Nature Kid's Guide to

LEMURS

DAVID ANDERSON

LP Media Inc. Publishing
Text copyright © 2026 by LP Media Inc.
All rights reserved.

For information address LP Media Inc. Publishing,
30012 Variolite St NW, Princeton MN 55371
www.lpmedia.org

Publication Data

Lemurs
The Nature Kid's Guide to Lemurs — First edition.

Summary: "Learn all about Lemurs, the Nature Kid Way"
— Provided by publisher.

ISBN: 979-8-89818-155-0

[1. Lemurs – Non-Fiction] I. Title.

Title: The Nature Kid's Guide to Lemurs

CONTENTS

MADAGASCAR'S MARVELS
DID YOU KNOW?
The word "lemur" comes from a Latin word meaning ghost or spirit — because of their spooky night calls and glowing eyes!
4

Whoop! A lemur leaps between branches in a misty forest.

Lemurs live on one island called Madagascar. This island sits near Africa, about 250 miles off the coast. No other place on Earth has wild lemurs.

Lemurs are primates, just like monkeys and apes. But they are much older than monkeys. They have soft fur and big, bright eyes that seem to glow in the dark. Those giant eyes help them see in the forest at night when most animals cannot!

More than 100 kinds of lemurs roam this island. Some are tiny enough to fit in your hand. Others are as big as a house cat. They all need the forest to survive.

TREE LIFE

A lemur's bottom front teeth stick out and work like a tiny comb for cleaning fur!

Thump! A lemur lands on a thick branch with a soft grip.

A lemur's body is built for life in the trees. Strong back legs help it jump far. Soft pads on its hands and feet grip the bark like shoes on a gym floor.

Most lemurs have long tails for balance. A lemur's wet nose picks up smells from far away, much better than your nose can. They can even sniff out which fruits are ripe and ready to eat before they take a single bite!

Lemurs have fingers and thumbs, just like you. They use them to grab food, hold branches, and groom their friends. Some lemurs even have a special extra-long finger just for digging bugs out of tree bark!

ISLAND LABORATORY

FUN FACT!

About 90% of Madagascar's plants and animals live nowhere else on Earth!

Rustle! Leaves shake as an old, old forest wakes up at dawn.

Madagascar broke away from Africa a long time ago. The animals on the island grew up all alone.

Lemurs had the forests to themselves. No monkeys or apes lived there to compete for food. So lemurs spread all over the island.

The trees, rivers, and mountains shaped each kind of lemur differently. Big lemurs grew in places where food was plentiful and easy to find. Small lemurs thrived where hiding and squeezing into tight spaces kept them safe. Some even learned to eat bamboo because it grew everywhere and nothing else wanted it!

STINKY TAILS

Pee-yew! A ring-tailed lemur waves its smelly tail at another lemur.

Ring-tailed lemurs live in groups led by females. The females get first pick of the food. They also choose where the group sleeps at night.

When two males want to fight, they have a stink battle instead of biting. Each one rubs smelly goo on his tail from special glands on his wrists. Then he waves it at the other lemur! The smelliest one usually wins.

But smell is not the only way ring-tailed lemurs communicate. They also howl, grunt, and purr. A loud call warns the whole group the moment danger is near.

FOSSA FEAR

A fossa can grow nearly six feet long from nose to tail. That's almost as long as your bed!

Hiss! A fossa creeps along a branch, hunting for lemurs.

The fossa is the biggest hunter on Madagascar. It looks like a small, slim cat with a long tail. It is fast, sneaky, and very dangerous.

Fossas climb trees just as well as lemurs do. They hunt both day and night, so lemurs are never truly safe. A fossa can chase a lemur through the trees at top speed, leaping from branch to branch.

When a sifaka spots a fossa, it screams a warning. The whole group runs and leaps away as fast as they can. Speed is their best way to stay safe.

A ring-tailed lemur's tail has exactly 13 black stripes and 13 white stripes!

DID YOU KNOW?

14

Purrr! A ring-tailed lemur stretches wide and soaks up the sun.

Ring-tailed lemurs love the sun. Each morning, they sit up with arms spread wide. They warm their bellies in the golden light, looking like tiny yoga masters.

These lemurs have black and white striped tails. A tail can be longer than its whole body! The bold stripes help the group stay together in tall grass.

Ring-tailed lemurs eat fruit, leaves, and flowers. They spend more time on the ground than most lemurs. That makes them easy to spot in the wild.

They are also one of the loudest animals in Madagascar, with calls strong enough to carry nearly half a mile!

EERIE AYE-AYES

An aye-aye's middle finger is so thin and bony, it looks like a skeleton finger!

Tap, tap, tap! An aye-aye knocks on a branch with one long finger.

The aye-aye is one of the strangest lemurs. It has huge ears, wild fur, and big yellow eyes. It comes out only at night, creeping through the dark forest.

An aye-aye taps on trees to find bugs hiding inside. It listens for hollow spots where grubs live. Then its long, bony middle finger digs the bugs out. No other primate hunts this way.

Some people on Madagascar fear the aye-aye. Old stories say it brings bad luck. But it is really a shy and harmless animal that just wants to eat bugs.

SINGING INDRIS

The indri is the only lemur with almost no tail — just a tiny 2-inch stub!

Eeee-ooo! An indri sings a loud song across the forest.

The indri is the biggest lemur alive today. It can weigh up to 20 pounds and stand as tall as a small child. Its black and white fur stands out in the green forest.

Indris sing to each other in loud, eerie calls. A family sings together every morning to say "this is our home." Their song can be heard two miles away!

Most lemurs jump from tree to tree. But the indri is one of the best leapers of all. It can sail 30 feet in a single bound, like a furry rocket.

SIFAKA SPRINGERS

Boing! A sifaka springs from trunk to trunk in the treetops.

Sifakas are named for the sound they make. "Shi-fak!" they cry when danger is near. This sharp call warns the whole group to run.

In the trees, sifakas push off with strong back legs. They can leap more than 20 feet between trunks. They twist in midair and land perfectly every time, making it look easy.

Sifakas eat leaves, bark, and fruit. They live in small family groups in the forest. Mothers carry babies on their bellies at first, then on their backs as they grow. The whole family helps watch over the little ones, taking turns keeping them safe and warm.

MIGHTY MOUSE!

Scientists keep finding new kinds of mouse lemurs — over 20 species discovered since the year 2000!

Squeak! A tiny mouse lemur darts across a branch at night.

The mouse lemur is the smallest primate in the world. Some weigh just one ounce — less than a slice of bread! Its big, round eyes take up most of its tiny face.

Mouse lemurs sleep all day in leaf nests or tree holes. At night, they wake up to hunt for insects and fruit. They move fast and are hard to spot in the dark.

When food is hard to find, mouse lemurs slow their bodies down. They use fat stored in their tails to stay alive. It is like having a built-in snack pack.

RUFFED LEMURS

Roaar! A ruffed lemur's scream echoes through the treetops.

The black and white ruffed lemur is one of the loudest lemurs. Its call is a deep, booming roar that sounds almost like a lion. You can hear it from very far away.

Ruffed lemurs are one of the only primates that build nests for their babies. The mother hides her young in the nest while she goes off to find food.

These lemurs love fruit and help spread seeds through the forest. When they eat, seeds fall to the forest floor. New trees grow where the seeds land. These lemurs are like furry gardeners!

BLUE-EYED BEAUTIES
DID YOU KNOW?
Humans and blue-eyed black lemurs are the only two primates in the world with true blue eyes!

Chirp! A blue-eyed black lemur calls out from a wet, green tree.

The blue-eyed black lemur has bright blue eyes. It is the only lemur with this eye color. Males have jet black fur, but females are reddish brown — they look like different animals!

These lemurs live in the wet forests of northwest Madagascar. They munch on fruit, nectar, and pollen. Sometimes they stick their faces deep into flowers to lick nectar, like tiny bears raiding honey.

Blue-eyed black lemurs are very rare. Only a few thousand live in the wild. They are one of the most endangered primates on Earth.

RUSTY ROARS

FUN FACT!
Red ruffed lemurs hang upside down by their feet to reach fruit — like furry acrobats!

Woooo! A red ruffed lemur howls loud enough to shake the trees.

Red ruffed lemurs have rusty red fur and black faces. They are one of the largest lemurs, weighing up to 9 pounds. A fluffy ruff of fur rings their neck like a fancy scarf.

These lemurs live high in the treetops. They rarely come to the ground. Fruit makes up most of their diet, and they travel far to find the ripest pieces.

Red ruffed lemurs live in only one small part of Madagascar. The forest they call home is getting smaller every year. People are working hard to protect them before it is too late.

HOPPING SIFAKAS

Hop, hop, hop! A Coquerel's sifaka bounces across open ground.

Coquerel's sifaka has white fur with big brown patches. It lives in the dry forests of western Madagascar. This lemur is easy to spot against the green leaves.

When it needs to cross open ground, it hops sideways on two feet. It holds its arms up high for balance. It looks exactly like it is dancing!

Coquerel's sifakas munch on leaves, flowers, and bark. They live in groups of up to ten. At night, they cuddle close on a branch to stay warm together.

BAMBOO BRAVERY
DID YOU KNOW?
Scientists did not discover the golden bamboo lemur until 1987 — it was hiding in plain sight!

Crunch! A bamboo lemur bites into a thick, green bamboo stalk.

Bamboo lemurs eat mostly bamboo. That may sound simple, but bamboo has poison in it called cyanide. These lemurs are one of the few animals that can eat it and not get sick.

A golden bamboo lemur eats enough cyanide each day to kill a human. It eats more poison than a much bigger animal ever could. Scientists still do not know how they survive!

Bamboo lemurs are small and quick. They grip bamboo stalks with strong hands and sharp teeth. They live deep in Madagascar's rain forests, hidden among the green stems.

WOOLLY WONDERS

Snuggle! A pair of woolly lemurs sit together on a branch.

Woolly lemurs have soft, thick fur. It looks like a cozy winter coat. They sleep curled up in tree holes all day and come out only at night.

These lemurs eat mostly leaves. They pick young, tender ones from high up in the trees. Their special stomachs can break down tough plants that other animals cannot eat.

Woolly lemurs live in pairs or small family groups. They are calm and quiet, rarely making loud calls. They do not move far from their sleeping tree, staying close to home.

CROWNED CLIMBERS

Crowned lemurs sometimes eat dirt and clay — it helps settle their stomachs like medicine!

Scratch! A crowned lemur scrambles up a tree with its orange crown.

Crowned lemurs get their name from the orange fur on their heads. It looks like a little crown! Males are grayish-brown and females are gray with brighter orange crowns.

These lemurs live in northern Madagascar. They move through dry forests in small groups, chattering as they go. They eat fruit, flowers, and sometimes insects.

Crowned lemurs are tough survivors. They can live in many types of forests. They even live on dry, rocky cliffs where few other lemurs dare to go.

FORESTS FALLING

Crack! A tree falls, and the forest grows a little smaller.

Almost all lemurs are in danger. People cut down forests to make farms and build homes. When trees go away, lemurs lose their homes and food.

Some lemurs, like the indri, cannot live anywhere else. If their forest is gone, they are gone too. Hunting and fires also hurt lemurs every year.

But there is hope. People around the world are trying to help. They plant trees, guard forests, and teach others why lemurs matter. Every small act can help save these amazing animals.

GLOSSARY

primate

An animal group that includes monkeys, apes, and humans.

canopy

The top layer of a forest, formed by the tallest trees and their branches

nocturnal

Active at night and asleep during the day

endemic

Found naturally in only one place on Earth and nowhere else

pollen

Tiny grains inside flowers that help new plants grow.